KEY STAGE 1

Year 1 | Term 1

Teaching and Learning

Science
Activity Book

Andrew Hodges

Alan Jarvis

Heather Monaghan

Every effort has been made to trace copyright holders and to obtain their permission for the use of copyright material. The authors and publishers will gladly receive information enabling them to rectify any error or omission in subsequent editions.

First published 2001

Letts Educational Ltd, The Chiswick Centre,
414 Chiswick High Road, London W4 5TF
Tel: 020 8996 3333
Fax: 020 8742 8390
www.letts-education.com

Text © Andrew Hodges, Alan Jarvis, Heather Monaghan

Series editor: Alan Jarvis
Designed, edited and produced by Gecko Limited, Cambridge
Cover design: Santamaria
Illustrations: Sami Sweeten

British Library Cataloguing-in-Publication Data
A CIP record for this book is available from the British Library

ISBN 1 84085 543 6

Printed in the UK

Letts Educational Ltd, a division of Granada Learning Ltd. Part of the Granada Media Group.

Contents

How to use this book

In this book you will learn about how sounds are made and how you hear them. You will also find out where light comes from and about the difference between light and dark. Then you will learn about pushes and pulls and how things move.

Look out for these.

We need light to see things in the dark.

The introduction tells you the most important thing to learn.

Swing your arms.

The pictures can give you new ideas.

Find out about the special meaning

The first word in each sentence in the boxes is a doing word. It tells you what you have to do.

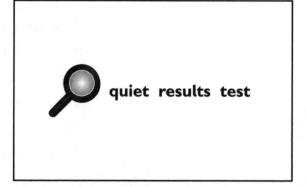

quiet results test

You need to know what the science words mean. Look these up on pages 44-46.

Sounds and hearing
You will learn:
- that there are many different sounds.
- about different ways of making and describing sounds.
- that you can make sounds by moving parts of your body.
- about how we hear sounds.
- that we hear with our ears.
- about some warning sounds and what they tell us.
- that some sounds can be heard from far away.
- that sounds get louder when you move closer to them.
- that sounds get quieter as they move further away.

Light and dark
You will learn:
- that we need light to see things.
- that there are many sources of light.
- that light sources can be bright or dim.
- that the Sun is the source of light for the Earth.
- that it is dangerous to look at the Sun because it is so bright.
- that other sources of light show up best at night-time.
- that we cannot see anything when it is really dark.
- that when it is dark we can use other senses to help us find things.
- that shiny things reflect light.
- that we only see shiny things when light shines on them.
- that shiny objects are not sources of light.

Pushes and pulls
You will learn:
- about different things that move.
- about different ways of making and describing movements.
- that pushing or pulling something can make it start or stop moving.
- that moving things can be dangerous.
- that it can be difficult to stop something that is moving fast.
- that some things move without anyone pushing or pulling them.

Lots of different things make sounds.

We often know what is making a sound even when we can't see it.

What sounds do these things make?

Talk about how these different things make sounds.
Do they move when they make a sound?

Everybody's voice sounds different.
Mrs Bell's class are trying to guess who is talking.

Play the game shown in the picture.
Make a tape of different sounds from around your school.
Can your class guess what the sounds are?

There are many different ways to make sounds.

You can shake, hit, blow or pluck these musical instruments.

You hit a drum.

You shake maracas.

You blow into a recorder.

You pluck guitar strings.

Collect some musical instruments to display in your classroom.

How do you make sounds with these instruments?

Talk about the different sounds these instruments make.
Make some sound-makers of your own.

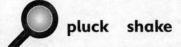 **pluck   shake**

Some sounds are high.
Some sounds are low.

These make high sounds.

These make low sounds.

Find ways of making high and low sounds with your instruments. How high and how low can you sing?

Which of these can make a loud sound?
Which make a rattling or a ringing sound?

maracas

finger cymbals

a drum

a tambourine

Listen to some music. Can you hear when the music is loud and when it is quiet?

 loud   quiet   rattling   ringing

We can make sounds by moving parts of our bodies.

singing

stamping

clapping

whistling

Try moving without making a sound.
Then try making a sound without moving!

Your face and throat move when you speak.
Your throat vibrates.

Feel your face and throat when you make loud and quiet sounds. Feel your throat when you sing. What happens when you sing higher and when you sing lower?

 loud   quiet   vibrate

Some sounds warn us of danger.

Why is this lorry making a warning sound?

The children stop and wait.

Talk about other sounds that warn us of danger.

Some sounds tell us to do something.

The siren is very noisy!

It's telling the cars to get out of the way.

When he blows the whistle, the players must stop.

Are there any sounds in your school that tell you things?

 **noisy**

We hear with our ears.

Mrs Bell's class cannot see her. Can they tell where she is when she claps her hands?

Try playing the game shown in the picture.
Do you need to see to be able to hear?

Do we need two ears to hear?
These children are trying to find out.

Sound Words

loud   banging
quiet   noisy
ringing   soft
rattling   high
clanging   low

Try this yourself. Can you think of other ways you can test your hearing? Try to find out how ears work.

 ears   test

We can hear some sounds that are far away.

How far away can you hear a very quiet sound?

Play this game with a friend. First, make the sound as far away as possible. If your friend cannot hear it, move closer.

Mrs Bell's class are playing a game to test this.

Ask lots of people to try the game.
Who is best at hearing really quiet sounds?
Make a chart to show the results of the game.

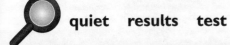 quiet   results   test

19

Sounds are quieter when they are far away.

The further away something is, the quieter it sounds.

Try this test yourself. Is the sound louder when you move closer? Is it quieter when you move away?

Can Clare follow the sound and get to the end of the maze?

Try this game with your friends.

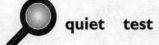 quiet   test

Some lights are bright. Some lights are dim.

There are lots of lights in this classroom.
They are all sources of light.
How many coloured lights can you see?

What lights can you see in your classroom?
Make a display of different lights.
Label the lights 'bright' or 'dim'.

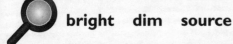

bright   dim   source

The Sun is the source of light for the Earth.

When it is day, there is light from the Sun.
You must never look at the Sun because its bright light will hurt your eyes.

Talk about what happens when clouds cover the Sun.
How can you tell how brightly the Sun is shining?

When it is night, there is much less light.

Talk about the differences between the two pictures.

 bright   day   eyes   night   source   Sun

When it is really dark, we cannot see anything.

Robin class are trying to make the classroom dark.

First, Mrs Bell switches off the lights in the classroom.

Next, Mrs Bell pulls down the blinds.

Try this in your classroom, or in a cupboard where you can make it really dark.

Then Mrs Bell draws the curtains.

Mrs Bell switches on a torch.

Talk about how you find things if it is really dark.

 dark

We need light to see things in the dark.

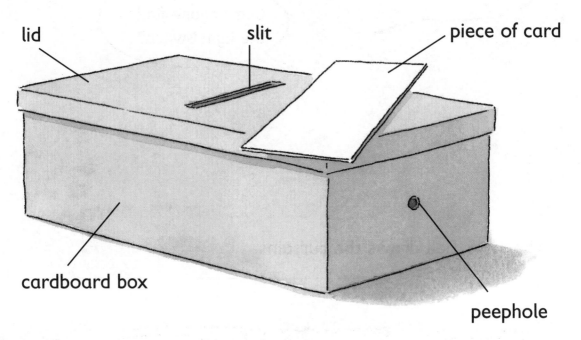

lid — slit — piece of card

cardboard box

peephole

There is something hidden inside this box.

Ed is trying to see what is inside.

He takes off the cardboard top so
that light can shine through the hole.

He needs more light to help him see.
So, he shines a torch through the hole.

Try this yourself and use lots of different torches.
Which torch worked best?
Make a collection of torches to display in your classroom.

 dark

We can see shiny things in the dark.

Shiny things reflect light. We can see them at night when light shines on them.

Cyclists wear reflective bands at night so that cars can see them.

Can you think of other shiny things that reflect light?

 night   reflect   reflective

31

We can see lights more clearly at night-time.

This is because it is dark at night. We can see other lights more clearly when the Sun isn't shining.

Hanukkah candles

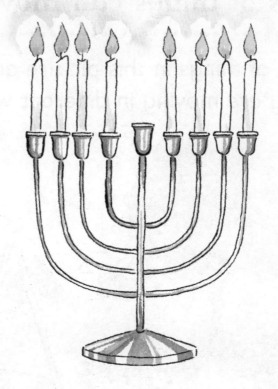

Christingle candle

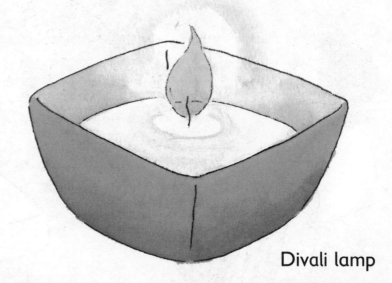

Divali lamp

Find out about the special meaning of these lights.

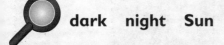 dark   night   Sun

Lots of things can move.

Lots of things in this picture are moving.
They are moving in different ways.

Things that move fast do not stop easily.

Talk about the way these things move.
Which are moving fast?

You can move your body in different ways.

Try moving like these children.

Shake your head.

Twist.

Hop.

Swing your arms.

Talk about which parts of your body moved.

We can tell people things without talking.

Stop!

Goodbye!

Be quiet!

Try playing this game. Move a part of your body and see if your friend can copy you. Take turns to copy each other.

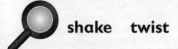 shake twist

We can move things by pushing and pulling them.

· ·

You can push a door to close it.
You can pull a drawer to open it.

Push up.

Pull down.

Pull at both ends.

Talk about the pushes and pulls you can see in the pictures.

Some toys move when you push or pull them.

Push along.

Pull along.

Push down.

Make a toy display. Label the toys 'push' or 'pull'.

 pull   push

It can be hard to stop things that are moving.

How can the children stop these sledges?

Think about which sledge will go faster down the hill.

Moving things can be dangerous.

This swing is going very high.

This cyclist is going very fast.

Talk about why these moving things are dangerous.
What can happen if you get too close to them?

Some things move without people pushing or pulling them.

No-one is pushing these things. What is moving them?

Look around your school for things that move without someone touching them. Draw some of them.

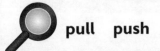 pull   push

Useful science words

bright   A bright light is a strong light that is easy to see.

dark   Without light.

day   It is day from sunrise to sunset. When it is day in Britain, it is night on the other side of the world.

dim   A dim light is not very bright, so it is difficult to see.

ears   The parts of your body that you use to hear things.

eyes   The parts of your body that you use to see things.

loud   A loud sound is easy to hear.

night   When it is night, we cannot see the Sun.

noisy   A noisy sound is loud and not very nice to listen to.

pluck   To pluck a string, you pull it and then let it go.

pull   You pull something towards you.

push   You push something away from you.

quiet   A quiet sound is not very loud, so it is difficult to hear.

rattling Some things make a rattling sound when you shake them. A baby's rattle makes a rattling sound.

reflect   To bounce back from the surface (outside or top part) of something.

reflective Good at reflecting light.

results   The results of a game or a test are the things that happen and that you find out.

ringing   Some things make a ringing sound when you hit or shake them. The sound is like a bell.

shake   To shake something, you move it up and down or from side to side.

source   The place where something begins or comes from. Light comes from a lamp, so the lamp is a source of light. A bell is a source of sound.

Sun   The source of light for the Earth.

test   A scientific way of finding out about something.

twist   You twist something to make it turn around.

vibrate   When something vibrates it shakes very quickly. If you put your hand on a washing machine when it is working, you can feel the machine vibrating.